W9-AUD-669

3 GO 00054421

DATE DUE

AUG 1 4 2006

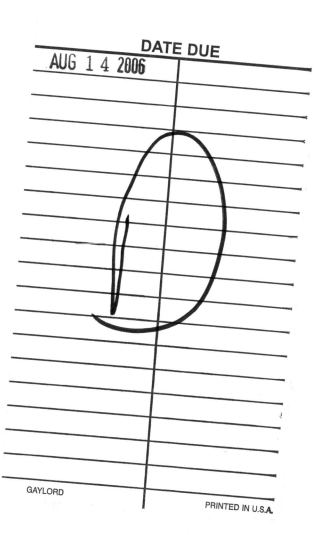

GAYLORD

PRINTED IN U.S.A.

Symbols, Landmarks, and Monuments

The

Pentagon

Tamara L. Britton

ABDO Publishing Company

visit us at
www.abdopub.com

Published by ABDO Publishing Company, 4940 Viking Drive, Edina, Minnesota 55435.
Copyright © 2003 by Abdo Consulting Group, Inc. International copyrights reserved in
all countries. No part of this book may be reproduced in any form without written
permission from the publisher.

Printed in the United States of America

Editors: Kate A. Conley, Kristy Langanki Cannon, Kristianne E. Vieregger
Photo Credits: AP/Wide World, Corbis, TimePix
Art Direction & Maps: Neil Klinepier

Library of Congress Cataloging-in-Publication Data

Britton, Tamara L., 1963-
   The Pentagon/ Tamara L. Britton.
     p. cm. -- (Symbols, landmarks and monuments)
   Includes index.
   Summary: Describes the design, construction, history, and renovation of the Pentagon,
the headquarters of the Department of Defense, as well as the terrorist attack on it on
September 11, 2001
   ISBN 1-57765-849-3
   1. Pentagon (Va.)--Juvenile literature. [1. Pentagon (Va.)] I. Title. II. Series.

UA26.A727 B75 2002
355.6'0973--dc21

2002025356

Contents

The Pentagon

The Pentagon is the center of American military power. This massive building houses the U.S. Department of Defense. The Pentagon is located in Arlington, Virginia, across the Potomac River from Washington, D.C.

Construction crews built the Pentagon during **World War II**. The war caused shortages of building materials. This challenged **architects** and construction crews. Despite the shortages, they completed the building after only 16 months of work.

For more than 50 years, the Pentagon has served the U.S. military. In 1991, workers began **renovating** the building. They wanted to make it safer and more modern.

The renovation went smoothly until September 11, 2001. That day, **terrorists** flew a plane into the Pentagon. The terrorist attack damaged part of the building. But construction crews continued the renovation and hope to complete it on time.

4

The Pentagon

Fun Facts

√ The Pentagon is so big that the U.S. Capitol could fit into any one of its five wedge-shaped sections.

√ In 1992, the Pentagon was designated a National Historic Landmark.

√ The Pentagon is the largest low-rise office building in the world. It is three times the size of the Empire State Building.

√ The Pentagon has 67 acres (27 ha) for parking.

√ Each side of the Pentagon is 921 feet (281 m) long.

√ The Pentagon has 131 stairways, 19 escalators, 13 elevators, 691 drinking fountains, and 7,754 windows.

√ Despite its massive size, the Pentagon's design allows workers to walk between any two places in the building in less than seven minutes.

√ The Pentagon's architects used building materials creatively and saved steel equal to the amount needed to build one World War II battleship.

Timeline

1941   √ Construction on the Pentagon begins on September 11.

1942   √ Construction crews complete the first two sections of the Pentagon.

1943   √ Construction crews complete the remainder of the Pentagon on January 15.

1955   √ A heliport is built at the Pentagon.

1976   √ The Office of the Secretary of Defense begins decorating corridors in the Pentagon to honor military heroes, U.S. presidents, and others.

1980s   √ New security measures are added to the Pentagon, including metal detectors and guard stations.

1991   √ President George H. W. Bush approves funding to renovate the Pentagon.

1994   √ Construction crews begin renovating the Pentagon's basement.

1998   √ Construction crews begin renovating Wedge 1.

2001   √ Wedge 1 renovation is complete.
       √ Terrorists fly an airplane into Wedge 1 on September 11.
       √ Reconstruction on Wedge 1 begins.

Planning the Pentagon

During **World War II**, 24,000 people worked for the U.S. War Department. They worked in more than 17 different buildings. This made it difficult for them to communicate, plan, and **strategize**.

Brigadier General Brehon B. Somervell thought all War Department employees should work in one building. So on July 17, 1941, Somervell asked **architect** George Edwin Bergstrom to design a building to house all War Department employees.

Somervell wanted Bergstrom to complete the plans quickly. So Bergstrom and a team of architects and engineers worked day and night on the building's design. They finished their plans on July 21, 1941. It had taken them less than four days to design the world's largest **low-rise** office building.

Brehon B. Somervell

9

Franklin D. Roosevelt

Bergstrom had faced many challenges in designing the building. The proposed site along the Potomac River in Arlington, Virginia, was made up of swampland and garbage dumps. In addition, five roads bound the site.

To fit in this challenging space, Bergstrom designed a three-story building with five sides. Each side was 921 feet (281 m) long. A five-sided shape is called a pentagon. That is how the Pentagon got its name.

The U.S. **Congress** approved the building's plans in the summer of 1941. Later that summer, President Franklin D. Roosevelt signed a bill approving money for the building.

Roosevelt feared that the new building would block the view of Washington, D.C., from Arlington National Cemetery. So he ordered the building to be constructed three-quarters of a mile (1 km) down the Potomac River from the proposed site.

Though the site had changed, the **architects** kept the building's design a pentagon shape. They thought the shape provided the most **efficient** use of space.

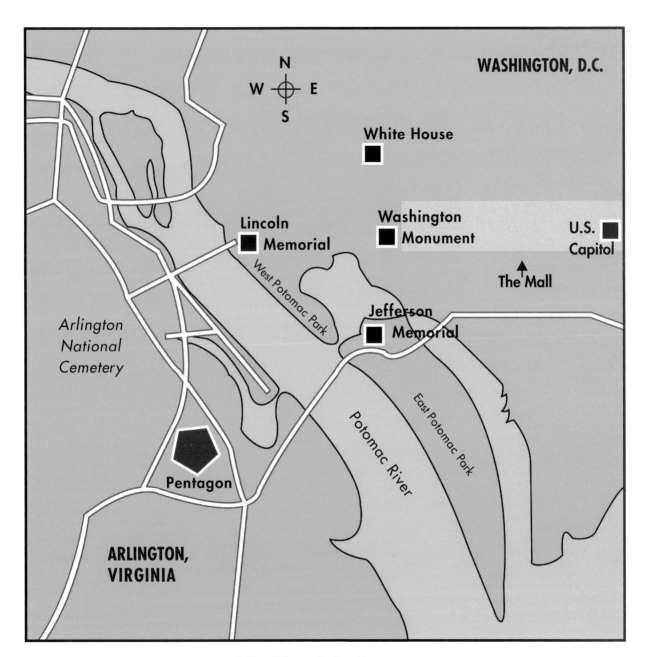

The Site of the Pentagon

Building the Pentagon

Construction on the Pentagon began on September 11, 1941. Then on December 7, 1941, Japan bombed Pearl Harbor, Hawaii. The attack drew the United States into **World War II**.

After the attack, planners added two more floors to the Pentagon. Construction crews worked hard to complete the building quickly. It would allow all War Department employees to manage the war from a central location.

During the war, little steel was available for construction projects. The United States used most of its steel to build ships, planes, and bullets. So workers built the Pentagon out of concrete. They **reinforced** the concrete with steel. This allowed the building to be strong without using too much valuable steel.

The Pentagon construction site

Construction crews work to complete the Pentagon.

A large Pentagon office

Planners saved steel in other areas, too. They chose to connect the floors with concrete **ramps** rather than elevators. They also used doors made of wood instead of steel.

About 15,000 workers labored night and day to finish the Pentagon as quickly as possible. Some workers filled in the swampland at the construction site with earth. Other workers used sand and gravel from the Potomac River to make concrete.

Workers used the concrete to make **pilings** for the building's **foundation**. Later, workers poured more concrete into wooden forms to make the building's walls. The Pentagon's outer walls were covered with limestone cut from a **quarry** in Indiana.

Workers completed the building's first two sections in the spring of 1942. On January 15, 1943, construction workers completed the rest of the Pentagon. In all, it took only 16 months to build. The project cost $83 million.

In 1942, War Department employees moved into the first completed sections of the Pentagon.

Center of U.S. Defense

The Pentagon is a symbol of U.S. military power. It is the headquarters of the Department of Defense. The department was created in 1949. It replaced the War Department. The Department of Defense trains and **equips** the military to defend the United States.

More than 23,000 people work at the Pentagon. The building covers 29 acres (12 ha) of land. It has 3.7 million square feet (344,000 sq. m) of office space.

The Pentagon is arranged in five **concentric** rings. Ring A is the Pentagon's innermost ring, and Ring E is its outermost ring. Ten corridors extend from Ring A to Ring E, like spokes on a bicycle wheel. A five-acre (2-ha) courtyard lies in the center of the building.

An entrance to the Pentagon

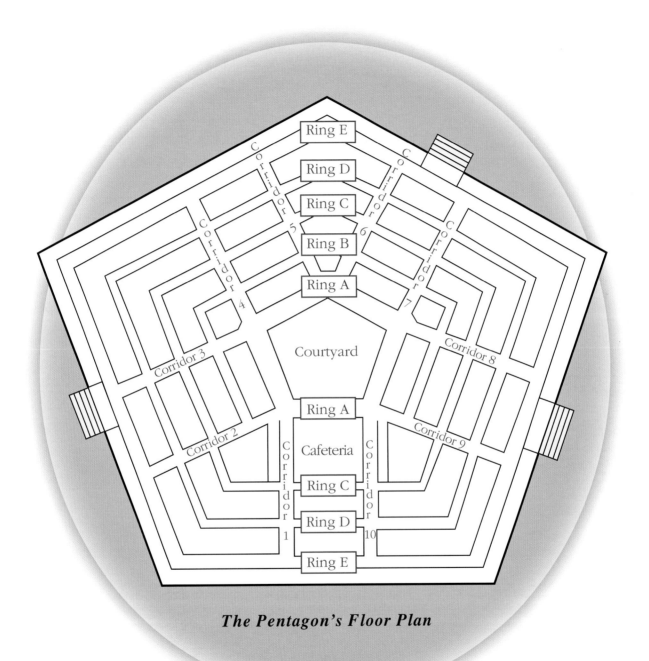

The Pentagon's Floor Plan

The Pentagon has five stories and two basement levels. The basement **concourse** has shops, restaurants, banks, and a clinic. Beneath the concourse are bus and taxi stations. The Pentagon has its own **heliport**, too.

Many top military leaders work at the Pentagon. The secretary of defense helps the president form U.S. defense policies. The chairman of the Joint Chiefs of Staff plans U.S. military operations. The Pentagon is also home to the secretaries of the army, navy, and air force.

U.S. military leaders have worked at the Pentagon for more than 50 years. From this building they directed **World War II**, the Korean War, the Vietnam War, and the Persian Gulf War.

But as time passed, the aging Pentagon no longer met all the current health and safety codes. And new technology, such as computers and fax machines, overwhelmed the old building. So officials decided to **renovate** the Pentagon.

Opposite page: Secretary of Defense Donald Rumsfeld (R) and Chairman of the U.S. Joint Chiefs of Staff Richard Myers (L) talk to reporters at the Pentagon.

Renovation

In 1991, President George H. W. Bush signed the Defense Authorization Act. It provided funds to **renovate** the Pentagon. The project would take 20 years and cost $1.2 billion.

Workers planned to strip down the building to its columns, floor, and outside walls. Then they would install new electric wiring, plumbing, and sprinkler systems. They also planned to **equip** the building to handle modern technology.

Workers began renovating the Pentagon's basement in 1994. They lowered the basement floor two feet (61 cm). This created enough space to add a **mezzanine** level.

Soon, workers began renovating the main floors of the Pentagon. To do this, they divided the Pentagon into five wedges. Each wedge would be renovated separately.

Renovation of Wedge 1 began in January 1998. Pentagon employees moved out of Wedge 1 and into nearby offices. Then construction crews **gutted** the wedge.

After construction crews gutted Wedge 1, only its most basic structure remained.

President George H. W. Bush approved the funding to renovate the Pentagon.

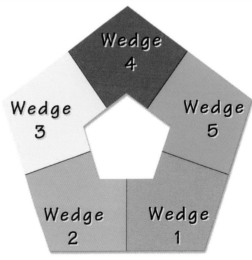

The Pentagon's Five Wedges

Gutting the wedge was a dangerous task. The wedge contained many harmful materials, such as **asbestos**. In all, crews removed 83 million pounds (38 million kg) of debris.

Next, construction crews began rebuilding Wedge 1. They added new steel **reinforcement** beams. The beams reached from the first floor all the way up to the fifth floor. These beams strengthened the wedge.

Construction crews placed Kevlar cloth between the beams. Kevlar is the material used in bulletproof vests. Planners hoped the Kevlar would stop flying debris if there were ever an explosion at the Pentagon.

Construction crews also replaced the old windows with glass that was two inches (5 cm) thick. Planners believed this special glass would not shatter easily during an explosion.

In all, construction crews **renovated** 1 million square feet (93,000 sq. m) of space in Wedge 1. On March 8, 2001, officials held a ribbon-cutting ceremony to open the newly renovated wedge. Pentagon workers began moving back into the offices in Wedge 1.

Colonel Robert Kirsch shows renovation work on Wedge 1 during a tour of the Pentagon in June 1999.

September 11, 2001

By the fall of 2001, Wedge 1 was almost fully occupied by Pentagon employees. Construction crews were finishing up details on the project. Soon, work would begin on Wedge 2.

Then on Tuesday, September 11, 2001, at 9:43 A.M., a plane slammed into the Pentagon. It was American Airlines Flight 77. The plane had taken off from Washington Dulles Airport and was headed for Los Angeles, California, when it crashed.

Employees at the Pentagon soon learned that two other planes had hit the World Trade Center's twin towers in New York City, New York. Yet another plane had crashed in a Pennsylvania field.

Later that day, President George W. Bush announced that the United States had been the victim of a **terrorist** attack. Terrorists had **hijacked** the four planes and used them as bombs to destroy symbols of American military and **economic** strength.

President George W. Bush (R), accompanied by Secretary of Defense Donald Rumsfeld (L), speaks in front of the Pentagon the day after the terrorist attack.

The plane that hit the Pentagon contained 20,000 gallons (76,000 liters) of fuel. That was enough fuel for the plane to fly across the country. The burning fuel created a fire that burned at more than 1,000 degrees Fahrenheit (538° C).

One hundred eighty-nine people died in the fire. Sixty-four of the victims had been onboard the plane. The other 125 victims were people who had been at the Pentagon. One hundred ten people were also wounded.

President Bush speaks during a memorial service at the Pentagon on October 11, 2001.

Thankfully, the plane had hit the newly **renovated** Wedge 1. The Kevlar cloth, sprinkler systems, and new windows installed during the renovation contained the damage.

Wedge 1 had the heaviest damage in Rings C, D, and E. Part of Ring E collapsed. Wedge 2 was also damaged. But the damage would have been much worse if the plane had hit an unrenovated wedge. Many more people might have lost their lives.

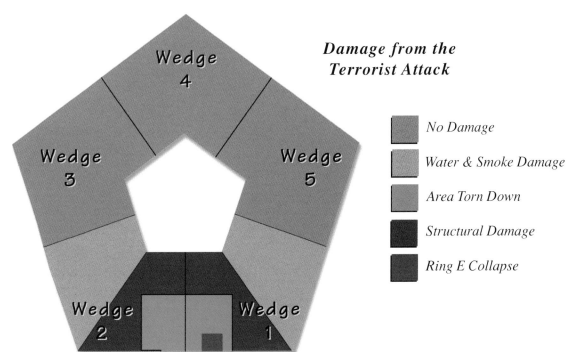

Damage from the Terrorist Attack

No Damage

Water & Smoke Damage

Area Torn Down

Structural Damage

Ring E Collapse

The Pentagon's Future

The crash site at the Pentagon was a Federal Bureau of Investigation (FBI) crime scene. The FBI released the site on September 26, 2001. Workers immediately began removing the more than 47,000 tons (43,000 t) of debris from the site.

Construction crews started rebuilding Wedge 1 in late November 2001. Officials wanted to rebuild the damaged areas of Wedge 1 to match the rest of the Pentagon. So they ordered limestone from the Indiana **quarry** that had provided the stone for the original construction.

FBI agents, firefighters, rescue workers, and engineers work together at the Pentagon crash site.

Pentagon officials expect Wedge 1 to be completed in 2003. The repair work will cost more than $700 million. Pentagon officials also plan to build a **memorial**. It will honor those who died in the attack.

Meanwhile, **renovation** work continues on the rest of the Pentagon. Despite the attack, officials and construction crews still hope to complete the Pentagon's renovation on schedule, in 2012. The renovation will make the Pentagon a safer place to work and visit for many years to come.

Construction crews must rebuild about 400,000 square feet (37,000 sq. m) of space that was damaged during the terrorist attack (L).

By December 11, 2001, construction crews had made major progress in repairing the Pentagon (R).

Glossary

architect - a person who plans and designs buildings.

asbestos - minerals that builders often used to fireproof buildings. Today, scientists know that breathing in asbestos fibers can cause cancer.

concentric - having a common center.

concourse - a large, open space in a building where crowds gather.

Congress - the lawmaking body of the United States. It is made up of the Senate and the House of Representatives. It meets in Washington, D.C.

economy - the way a nation uses its money, goods, and natural resources.

efficient - wasting little time or energy.

equip - to provide.

foundation - an underlying support structure or base in a building.

gut - to tear down the inside of a building.

heliport - a place for a helicopter to take off and land.

hijack - to overtake a vehicle, such as an airplane, by threatening the pilot with violence.

low-rise - having only a few stories.

memorial - something that stands as a reminder of a person or event.

mezzanine - a story in a building. A mezzanine often has a low ceiling and is usually located between two main stories.

piling - a beam driven into the ground to support a building.

quarry - a place where stone is dug, cut, or blasted out.

ramp - a sloping path connecting two different stories in a building.

reinforce - to strengthen by adding additional materials.

renovate - to restore or make new by rebuilding or repairing.

strategize - to plan and direct military operations.

terrorist - a person who uses violence to threaten people or governments.

World War II - 1939 to 1945, fought in Europe, Asia, and Africa. The United States, France, Great Britain, the Soviet Union, and their allies were on one side. Germany, Italy, Japan, and their allies were on the other side. The war began when Germany invaded Poland. The United States entered the war in 1941 after Japan bombed Pearl Harbor, Hawaii.

Web Sites

Would you like to learn more about the Pentagon? Please visit **www.abdopub.com** to find up-to-date Web site links about the Pentagon's history and renovation. These links are routinely monitored and updated to provide the most current information available.

Index